0
zero

null

10
ten

zehn

20
twenty

zwanzig

30
thirty

dreißig

40

forty

vierzig

50

fifty

fünfzig

60

sixty

sechzig

70

seventy

siebzig

80

eigthy

achtzig

90

ninety

neunzig

100

one hundred

einhundert

1000

one thousand

eintausend

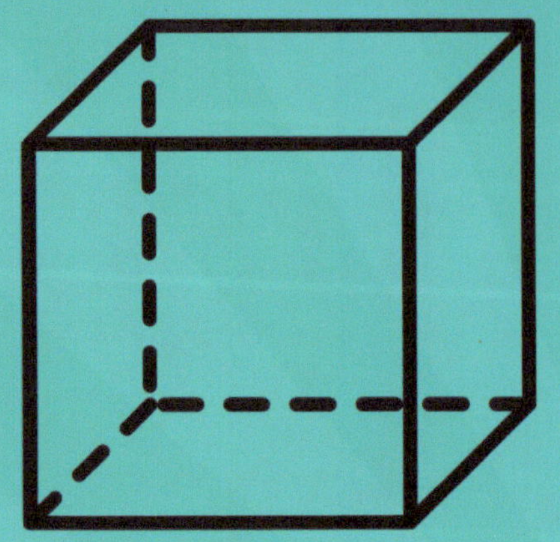

cube

Würfel

block

Spielbaustein

ice cube

Eiswürfel

caramel

Karamell

sugar

Zucker

dice

Würfel

gift box

Geschenkbox

cardboard box

Pappkarton

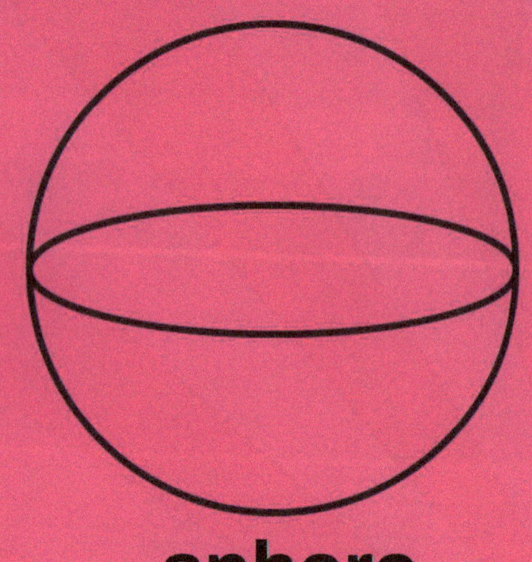

sphere

Kugel

ice cream scoop

Eiskugel

pearl

Perle

bubble

Blase

marbles

Murmeln

planet

Planet

snowball

Schneeball

tennis ball

Tennisball

cylinder

Zylinder

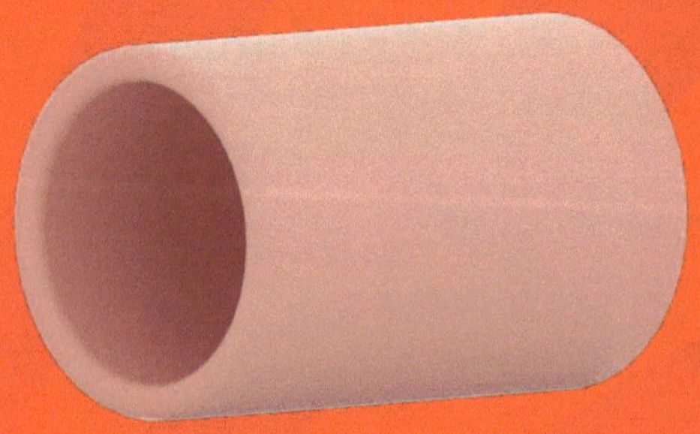

tube

Rohr

batteries

Batterien

thread spool

Garnspule

cinnamon

Zimt

rolling pin

Nudelholz

sausage

Wurst

hay bale

Heuballen

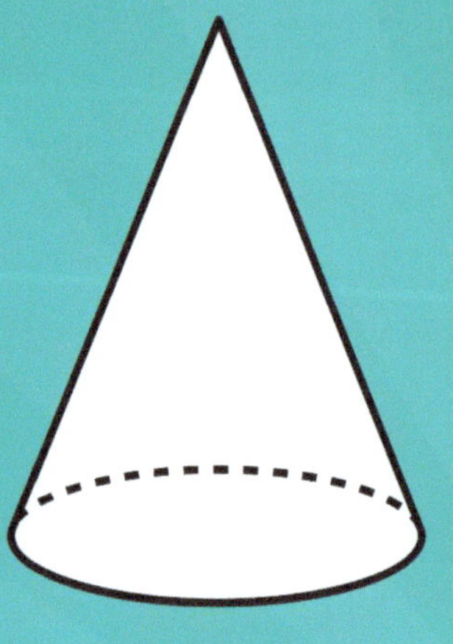

cone

Kegel

road cone

Verkehrskegel

ice cream cone

Eiswaffel

witch hat

Hexenhut

dungeon

Kerker

fir tree

Tannenbaum

party hat

Partyhut

snail

Schnecke

blackberry

Brombeere

currant

Johannisbeere

clementine

Clementine

durian

Durian

dragon fruit

Drachenfrucht

jackfruit

Jackfrucht

star fruit

Sternfrucht

asparagus

Spargel

radish

Radieschen

red bean

rote Bohne

turnip

Rübe

cassava

Maniok

sweet potato

Süßkartoffel

chickpeas

Kichererbsen

eagle

Adler

bat

Fledermaus

beaver

Biber

flamingo

Flamingo

raven

Rabe

blackbird

Amsel

blue tit

Blaumeise

magpie

Elster

swallow bird

Schwalbe

lark

Lerche

parakeet

Sittich

woodpecker

Specht

peacock

Pfau

parrot

Papagei

toucan

tukan

stork

Storch

coral

Koralle

sea anemone

Seeanemone

sea urchin

Seeigel

seahorse

Seepferdchen

clownfish

Clownfisch

goldfish

Goldfisch

crab

Krabbe

hermit crab

Einsiedlerkrebs

dolphin

Delfin

narwhal

Narwal

octopus

Oktopus

squid

Tintenfisch

whale shark

Walhai

orca

Orca

blue whale

Blauwal

beluga whale

Belugawal

hammerhead shark

Hammerhai

white shark

Weißer Hai

lemon shark

Zitronenhai

tiger shark

Tigerhai

grasshopper

Heuschrecke

caterpillar

Raupe

scorpion

Skorpion

lizard

Eidechse

dinosaurs

Dinosaurier

black hair

schwarzes Haar

ginger hair

rotes Haar

brown hair

braunes Haar

blond hair

blondes Haar

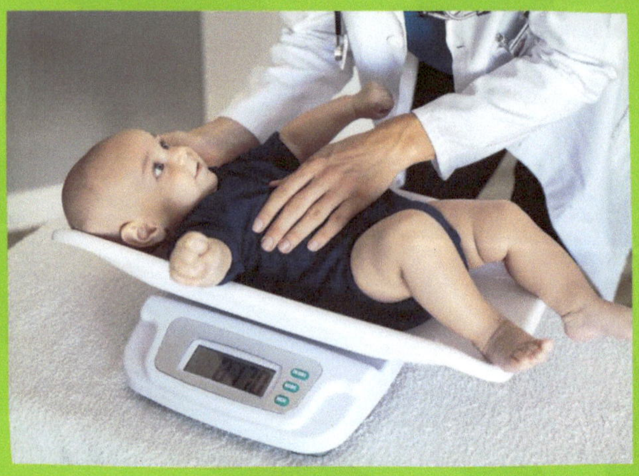

scale

Waage

hospital

Krankenhaus

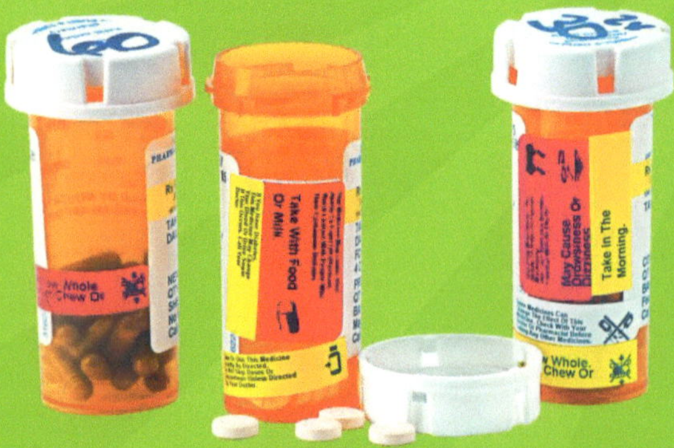

medicine

Medizin

thermometer

Thermometer

bandage

Verband

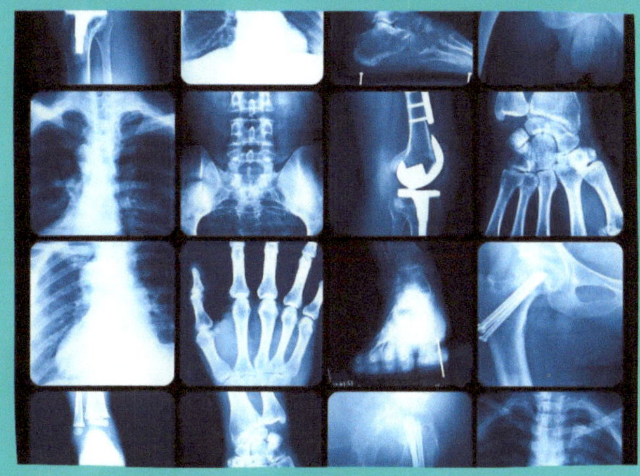

x-ray

Röntgen

doctor

Doktor

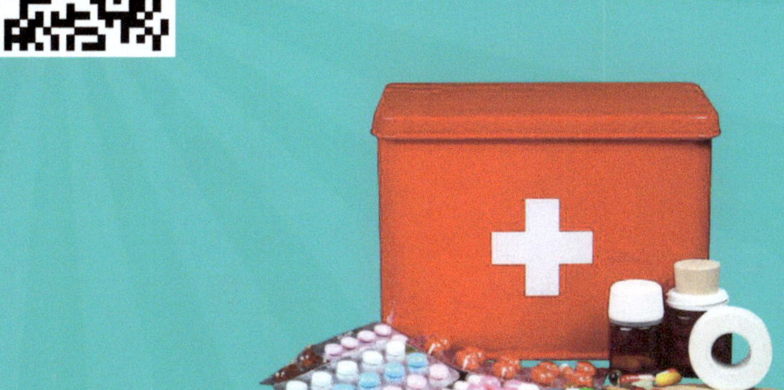

first aid kit

Erste-Hilfe-Kasten

play

spielen

draw

zeichnen

count

zählen

write

schreiben

dancing

Tanzen

swimming

Schwimmen

skiing

Skifahren

basketball

Basketball

tennis

Tennis

ping pong

Tischtennis

soccer

Fußball

horse riding

Reiten

ice hockey

Eishockey

judo

Judo

boxing

Boxen

running

Laufen

baseball

Baseball

cricket

Kricket

rugby

Rugby

volleyball

Volleyball

maracas

Maracas

tambourine

Tamburin

xylophone

Xylophon

violin

Geige

piano

Klavier

guitar

Gitarre

cello

Cello

harp

Harfe

drum

Trommel

djembe

Djembe

drum kit

Schlagzeug

trumpet

Trompete

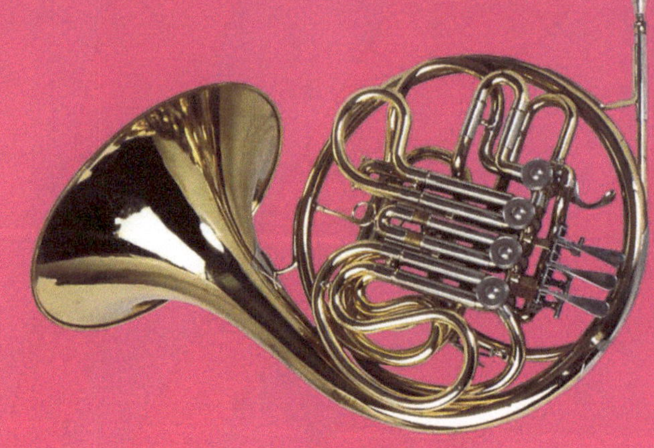

horn

Horn

saxophone

Saxophon

flute

Flöte

headphone

Kopfhörer

sing

singen

sheet music

Notenblatt

microphone

Mikrofon

www.ingramcontent.com/pod-product-compliance
Lightning Source LLC
LaVergne TN
LVHW071649180726
843512LV00002B/416